ADOLF HITLER
WHAT STARTED WORLD WAR 2

Biography 6th Grade
Children's Biography Books

BABY PROFESSOR
EDUCATION KIDS

Speedy Publishing LLC

40 E. Main St. #1156

Newark, DE 19711

www.speedypublishing.com

Copyright 2017

Adolf Hitler was a German Dictator from 1933 to 1945 who was known for starting World War II as well as the Holocaust. He was born in Braunau am Inn, Austria-Hungary on April 20, 1889 and he died in Berlin, Germany on April 30, 1945. Read further to learn about his power and rule as well as his demise.

WHERE DID HE GROW UP?

He was born in Austria, but his family would move around, and he lived in Germany for a short time and then moved back to Austria. He had an unhappy childhood. His parents both passed away at a fairly young age, as did many of his sisters and brothers.

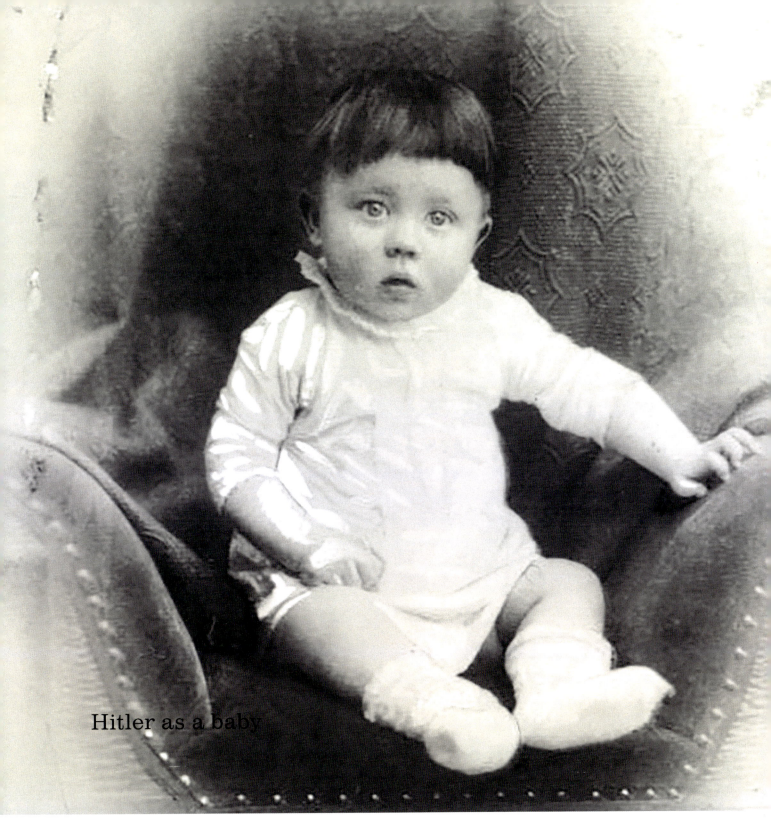

Hitler as a baby

H itler did not do so great in school, and was expelled from a couple of schools prior to moving to Vienna, Austria in pursuit of his dream to become an artist.

Adolf Hitler's School

He soon realized that he didn't have much talent and became very poor. He later moved to Munich, Germany, hoping to become an architect.

WORLD WAR I

Hitler signed up for the German army once WWI began. He was twice awarded the Iron Cross for his bravery. It was during this war that he discovered his love for war as well as becoming a strong German patriot.

World War 1

Treaty of Versailles Signing

POWER

Once the war was over, he decided to enter politics. Many Germans became upset over losing the war. In addition, they were not happy about the Treaty of Versailles, which, in addition to blaming the war on Germany, also took some of Germany's land.

During this same time period, Germany was now in an economic depression and many people were now poor. Because of the Treaty of Versailles and the economic depression, it was now time for Hitler's rise in power.

Signing of the Treaty of Versailles

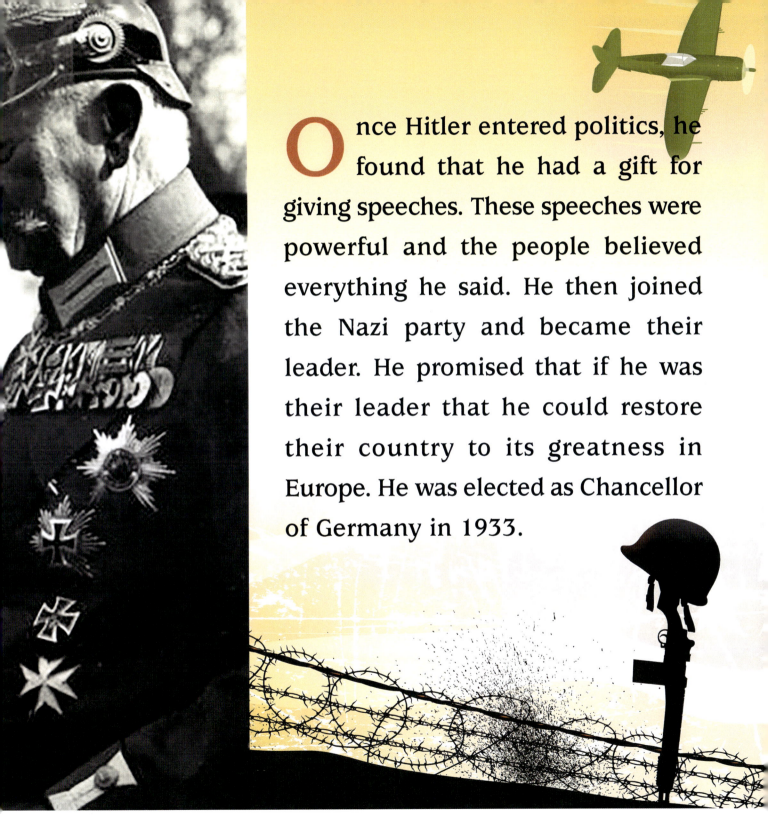

Once Hitler entered politics, he found that he had a gift for giving speeches. These speeches were powerful and the people believed everything he said. He then joined the Nazi party and became their leader. He promised that if he was their leader that he could restore their country to its greatness in Europe. He was elected as Chancellor of Germany in 1933.

There was no stopping him once he became Chancellor. He had studied Benito Mussolini of Italy, who had become his idol, to learn about installing a fascist government and becoming a dictator. He was soon the dictator of Germany.

Benito Mussolini

World War II

WORLD WAR II

For Germany to be able to grow, Hitler felt that they needed additional land or "living space". His first step was the annex of Austria to be a part of Germany, and he then overtook part of Czechoslovakia. However, this was not enough for Hitler.

Germany invaded Poland on September 1, 1939, and this was the beginning of World War II. He proceeded to form an alliance with the Axis Powers of Italy and Japan. They fought against the Allied Powers of the United States, the Soviet Union, France, and Britain.

US Troops

World War II

itler's army started taking over most of Europe. They quickly attacked in what became known as the Blitzkrieg or "lightning war". Germany was soon able to capture much of Europe that included Belgium, Denmark, and France.

The Allied, however, fought back. They invaded the beaches of Normandy on June 6, 1944, and were soon liberated by France. The Allies defeated most of Germany's army by March of 1945, and Hitler committed suicide on April 30, 1945.

Normandy

Adolf Hitler

LEADERS OF THE AXIS POWERS

Dictators ruled over the three major countries of the Axis Powers. They included:

- **Germany:** Adolf Hitler became Germany's Chancellor in 1933 and he became Fuhrer in 1934. He despised Jewish people and was a ruthless dictator. He wanted to rid Germany of all its weak people and desired control over all of Europe.

- **Italy:** Benito Mussolini was Italy's supreme dictator. He instituted the idea of a fascist government which consisted of one leader and one party retaining total power. He was also known to be Hitler's inspiration.

Benito Mussolini

Emperor Hirohito

- **Japan:** Emperor Hirohito's reign as the Emperor of Japan was from 1926 to 1989. He was retained as Emperor following the war. His subjects did not hear his voice until he announced on the radio about Japan's surrender.

LEADERS OF THE ALLIED POWERS

- **Great Britain:** Winston Churchill was Great Britain's Prime Minister during most of WWII, and was known as a great leader. Great Britain was the final county to fight against the Germans. He is remembered for his famous speeches as the Germans were bombing them at the Battle of Britain.

Winston Churchill

Franklin Roosevelt

● **United States:** Franklin D. Roosevelt was known to be one of the greatest presidents in United States' history. As President, he let the U.S. out of its Great Depression and throughout the battle of WWII.

● **Russia:** Joseph Stalin was the General Secretary of the Communist Party. He led his country through devastating and terrible battles with Germany, during which millions and millions died. After they won the war, he created the Eastern Bloc of Soviet led communist states.

Joseph Stalin

Charles de Gaulle

○ France: Charles de Gaulle was the leader of the Free French, and he led France's resistance movement against Germany.

THE HOLOCAUST

Hitler was known to be responsible for many of the most horrific crimes to be committed in history. He loathed the Jewish people and sought to eliminate them from his country. He made the Jewish people go to concentration camps, where six million were killed during WWII. In addition, he killed others he didn't like, including people of other races as well as handicapped people.

Concentration Camp During The Holocaust

World War I

WHY DID IT HAPPEN?

He despised the Jewish population and held them responsible for Germany losing WWI. He believed them to be less than human and he also was a believer of the dominance of the Aryan race and wanted to create a race of people that were perfect by using Darwinism and breeding.

In his book, Mein Kampf, Hitler wrote that once he became ruler he would purge Germany of all of the Jews. Only a few believed he would actually do this, but once he became Chancellor, it became apparent he would do this as he began his efforts against the Jews.

He created laws that stated Jews would have no rights, and he then organized attacks on Jewish homes and businesses. Many Jewish businesses and homes were vandalized or burnt down on November 9, 1938. This was known as the Kristallnacht, or the "Night of Broken Glass".

Krakow Ghetto

GHETTOS

As World War II went on, the Nazis would proceed in taking over a city in Europe and force the Jewish population into a certain part of town. This area was referred to as the ghetto and was guarded and fenced with barbed wire. There was little water, medicine or food available. In addition, it was crowded and multiple families would sometimes have to share a single room for living.

THE CONCENTRATION CAMPS

All of the Jewish population eventually were brought to these concentration camps. They would be told they were taking them to a better and new place, but that would not be the case. These concentration camps were similar to prison camps.

Concentration Camp

eople had to perform hard labor. The weak would quickly be killed or would die from starvation. Some of the camps would have gas chambers where people would be led to in big groups to die from the poisonous gas. These concentration camps were despicable places.

HIDING

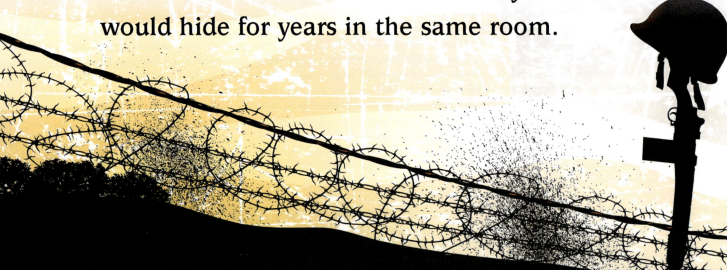

Many of the Jewish people would hide from the Nazis. They would sometimes hide with families that were not Jewish, or sometimes they might pretend to a part of a family, and then sometimes they would hide in a basement, attic, or hidden room. Eventually, some were able to escape and cross the border to a free country, but still some would hide for years in the same room.

World War II Injured Soldiers Being Evacuated

HOLOCAUST STORIES AND HEROES

There are several stories of the Jewish population attempting to survive during the Holocaust as well as the heroes that helped them. Here are just a few:

- Anne Frank's Diary
- Schindler's List
- The Hiding Place

Anne Frank's Diary – Her diary tells her real-life story as a young girl in hiding from the Nazis. She, along with her family, hid for two years before they were deceived and captured. She died while in a concentration camp, however, her diary lived on to tell her story.

Anne Frank School Photo

Oskar Schindler's Factory

Schindler's List – This movie reveals Oskar Schindler's story. He was a German businessman that would manage to save the lives of more than a thousand Jewish people that worked at his factories. Please note that this movie has an R rating and is not intended for children.

The Hiding Place – Corrie ten Boom's story, who was a Dutch lady that assisting in hiding Jewish people. However, she did get caught by a spy and was sent to a camp. She managed to survive the concentration camp and was let free when the war ended.

Ten Boom Museum

End of World War II

This was a horrible time for the Jewish people, and for everyone else that was not a part of Hitler's regime. Can you imagine being forced to live in one of these concentration camps or having to live in hiding for several years? For additional information about Adolf Hitler and the Holocaust, you can go to your local library, research the internet, and ask questions of your teachers, family and friends.

Made in the USA
Las Vegas, NV
11 December 2020